TiME ZONES

by David A. Adler

illustrated by Edward Miller

HOLIDAY HOUSE / NEW YORK

hat time is it?

In Los Angeles, California, it's 6 o'clock Thursday morning.
Adam, who lives there, is asleep.

But it's not 6 o'clock Thursday morning everywhere.

While Adam is sleeping . . .

zzZZ!

Los Angeles,
California,
USA

Maria, who lives in Buenos Aires, Argentina, is already in school. It's 11 o'clock Thursday morning in Buenos Aires.

Mohammed, who lives in Casablanca, Morocco, is still in school; but his school day is almost done. It's 2 o'clock Thursday afternoon in Casablanca.

Judith, who lives in Tel Aviv, Israel, is home from school. It's 4 o'clock Thursday afternoon in Tel Aviv.

Rajini, who lives in Bangkok, Thailand, will soon be going to sleep. It's 9 o'clock Thursday night in Bangkok.

Elizabeth, who lives in Sydney, Australia, is also sleeping. It's 1 o'clock Friday morning in Sydney.

The time is different in different parts of the world because the earth does not remain still. It slowly rotates.

Buenos Aires,
Argentina

Casablanca,
Morocco

Tel Aviv,
Israel

Bangkok,
Thailand

zzZZ!

Sydney,
Australia

If it's morning where you live, your place on Earth is rotating toward the sun. As the earth rotates, there's a time the sun is directly above where you live. That's midday in your part of the world. But when it's midday for you, halfway around the world it's midnight.

MIDNIGHT

NOON

12:00

Because the earth rotates in an easterly direction, the sun is directly over the east coast of the United States before it's over the west coast. It's noon in Miami, Florida, before it's noon in Portland, Oregon.

THE EARTH ROTATES THIS WAY!

● Portland, OR

Miami, FL ●

Many years ago, in the time of George Washington, each town had an official clock. The time was set so when the sun was directly overhead, it would be noon. People set their watches and clocks to be the same as the town clock. Of course, when it was noon in one place, it might be ten minutes before noon or ten minutes after noon in a town just one hundred miles away. When travelers came to a new town, they would reset their watches.

George Washington lived before the advent of the telegraph and telephone. People didn't travel much; and when they did, it was by horse and wagon and not on any real set schedule. The different times from one place to the next were not much of a problem.

OFFICIAL CLOCK

GEORGE WASHINGTON

But by the early 1800s, people began traveling by train, and they needed schedules. Trains traveled through many towns. Which town clock would set the time for the schedule? How would people in other towns know when to expect trains to arrive?

Railroad companies decided to end the confusion by setting standard times and time zones in the United States and Canada in 1883.

What about the rest of the world?

SPRINGFIELD

ST. LOUIS

chicago

Kalamazoo

COLUMbUS

Pittsburgh

NEXT TRaiN TO PiTTSbURgh LEaVES TOMORROW

WaiT!

International Meridian Conference • Washington, D.C., 1884

By the late 1800s, long-distance travel and communication became commonplace. People needed to know the time not only where they were, but in other places too.

In 1884, at a meeting in Washington, D.C., representatives from more than twenty countries divided the world into twenty-four time zones.

With time zones, when the sun is directly over a city, it's always noon or close to it. As you travel west, each time you cross the imaginary line between one time zone and the next, it becomes one hour earlier on the clock. As you travel east, each time you cross the imaginary line between one time zone and the next, it becomes one hour later.

West

East

Where are those imaginary lines between one time zone and the next? There's an imaginary circle, the equator, that runs midway between the North and South Poles. Circles are divided into 360 degrees. If you divide 360 by 24, the number of hours in a day, you get 15. The imaginary lines separating time zones are 15 degrees apart.

But where is the beginning point?

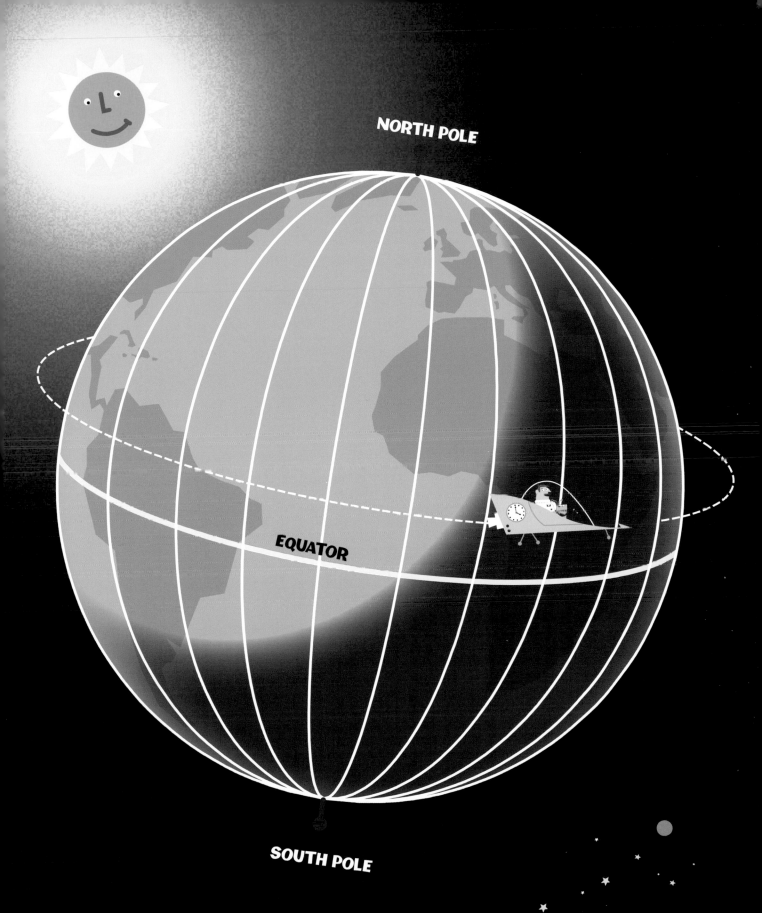

NORTH POLE

EQUATOR

SOUTH POLE

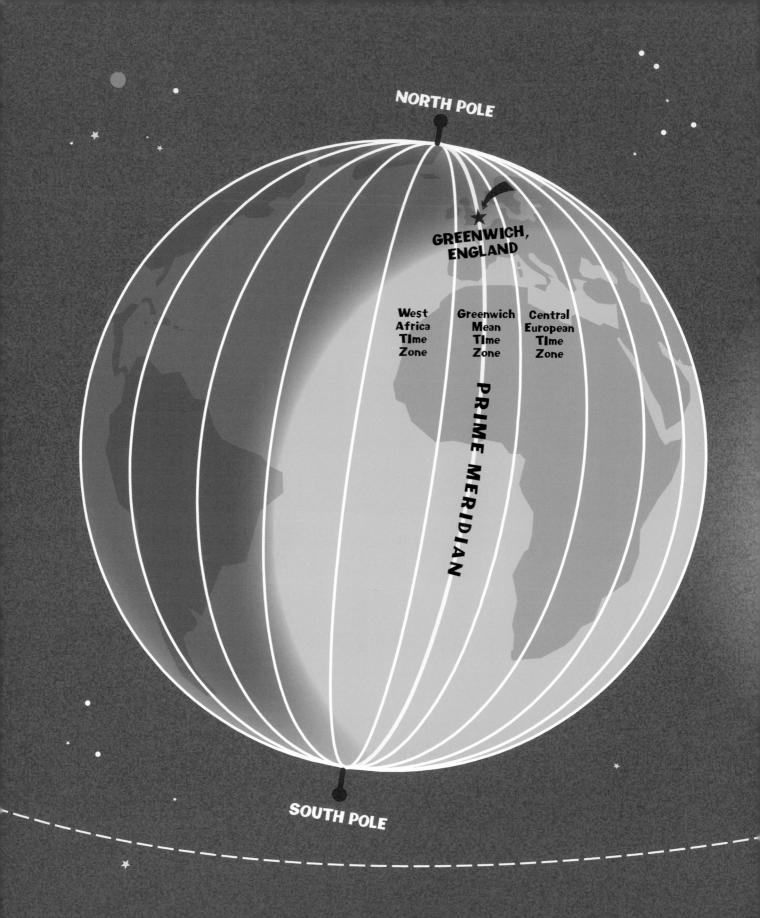

NORTH POLE

GREENWICH, ENGLAND

West Africa Time Zone

Greenwich Mean Time Zone

Central European Time Zone

PRIME MERIDIAN

SOUTH POLE

At the 1884 meeting, the imaginary line that goes through Greenwich, England, was made the beginning point and called the prime meridian.

Time zones have been given names, and the prime meridian runs through the middle of the Greenwich Mean Time Zone. It's an hour later on clocks in the time zone to the east, the Central European Time Zone. It's an hour earlier on clocks in the time zone to the west, the West Africa Time Zone.

| Paris | Tel Aviv | Moscow | New Delhi | Bangkok | Beijing |

Time zone lines are approximate. Time zones shown on clocks were calculated in mid-December, during Standard Time in the United States. Time differences between countries are not the same throughout the year because not all countries adopt Daylight Savings Time, and even those that do don't all adopt it at the same time.

Moscow, Russia

Tel Aviv, Israel

New Delhi, India

Beijing, China

Tokyo, Japan

Bangkok, Thailand

North
West ← → East
South

It would be confusing if an imaginary time zone line went through the middle of a city or through the middle of a small country. It would be confusing if on one side of town the time was 8:00 a.m. and on the other side it was 9:00 a.m. Imagine leaving for school at 8:00 a.m., crossing into a new time zone, and arriving just ten minutes later at 9:10 a.m. and being marked late! To avoid dividing cities and heavily populated areas into more than one zone, time zones are not always perfectly straight. But no matter how the lines zig and zag, as you travel west you set your clock back. As you travel east you set your clock ahead.

Time zone lines zig and zag, and in some parts of the world they bend a lot so it's the same time everywhere in a country. China and India are huge, but each of those countries has just one time zone.

What if you traveled around the world? What if you traveled west and circled the earth in exactly twenty-four hours? If you left your hometown at noon on Monday and each time you crossed into a new time zone you set your watch back one hour, at the end of your trip, according to your watch, it would still be noon on Monday!

But it's not noon on Monday. Twenty-four hours have passed. It's noon on Tuesday.

On your trip west you crossed the international date line, an imaginary line in the middle of the Pacific Ocean. It's 180 degrees from the prime meridian, halfway around the world. When you cross it traveling west, you add one day. When you cross it traveling east, you subtract one day.

International Date Line

WHAT DAY IS IT, ANYWAY?

IT'S MONDAY. NO, IT'S TUESDAY!

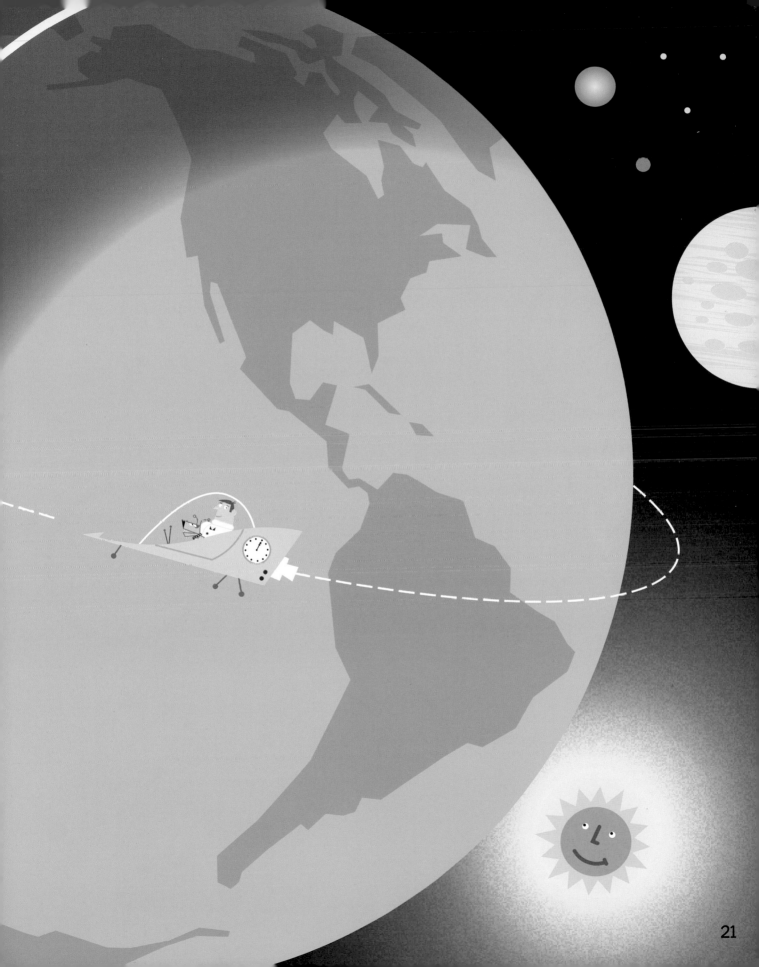

Do you have friends or family who live far from you?

Do you ever text or instant message people who live far away? If you do, ask them what time it is. It might be noon where you are and early in the morning or late at night where they are.

Denver

It's 5:00 p.m. in Casablanca.

It's 6:00 a.m. in Sydney.

It's 12:00 p.m. in D.C.

London

12:00

Have you ever traveled in a jet? Often, if you travel a great distance, the flight attendant will remind you to reset your watch. That's because you went from one time zone to another.

You may be surprised after a long flight across many time zones. If you fly west and set your watch back one hour each time you cross a time zone, according to your watch you might arrive before you left!

When you understand time zones, you understand why sometimes when you travel you have to reset your watch. You understand why it's noon on one side of the world and midnight on the other side. You understand why at the very same moment the time, maybe even the day, is different for Adam, Maria, Mohammed, Judith, Rajini, and Elizabeth.

United States Time Zones

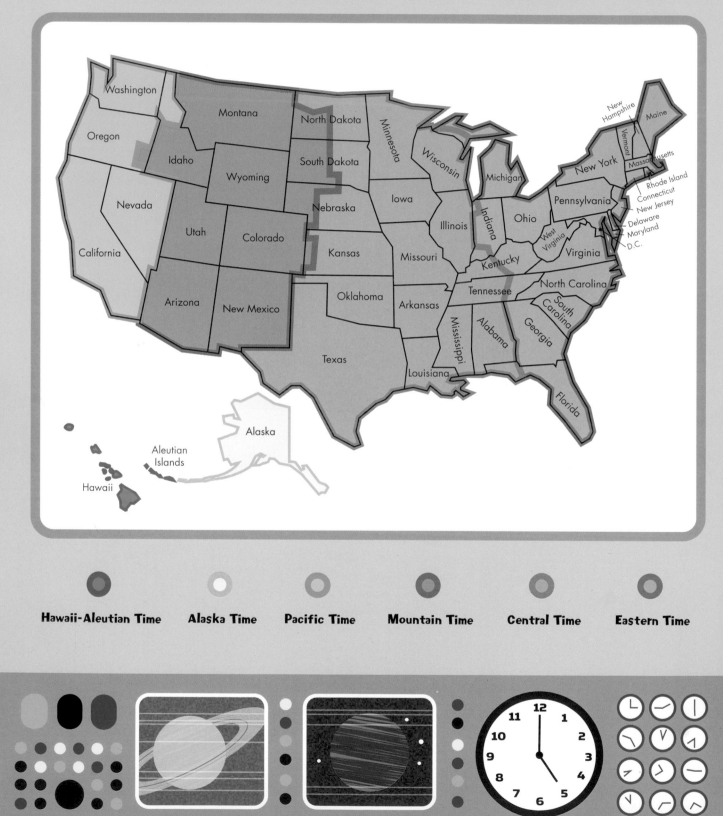

Washington, Oregon, Montana, Idaho, Wyoming, North Dakota, South Dakota, Minnesota, Wisconsin, Michigan, Nevada, Utah, Colorado, Nebraska, Iowa, Illinois, Indiana, Ohio, California, Kansas, Missouri, Kentucky, West Virginia, Virginia, Arizona, New Mexico, Oklahoma, Arkansas, Tennessee, North Carolina, Texas, Mississippi, Alabama, Georgia, South Carolina, Louisiana, Florida, New Hampshire, Maine, Vermont, New York, Massachusetts, Rhode Island, Connecticut, Pennsylvania, New Jersey, Delaware, Maryland, D.C.

Alaska, Aleutian Islands, Hawaii

Hawaii-Aleutian Time Alaska Time Pacific Time Mountain Time Central Time Eastern Time

Daylight Savings Time

The times in different parts of the world were calculated in mid-December, when the U.S. observes Standard Time. The time differences on clocks from city to city and country to country do change because of Daylight Savings Time.

Daylight Savings Time is observed in the U.S. in spring and summer because of the many hours of sunlight. Sunrise is early, while most people in the country are asleep. Rather than "waste" the sunlight, clocks are moved ahead one hour. That way the sun is shining one hour less when most people are still asleep and one hour more when most people are awake. Daylight Savings Time is not observed everywhere, and the start and end of Daylight Savings Time varies from place to place.

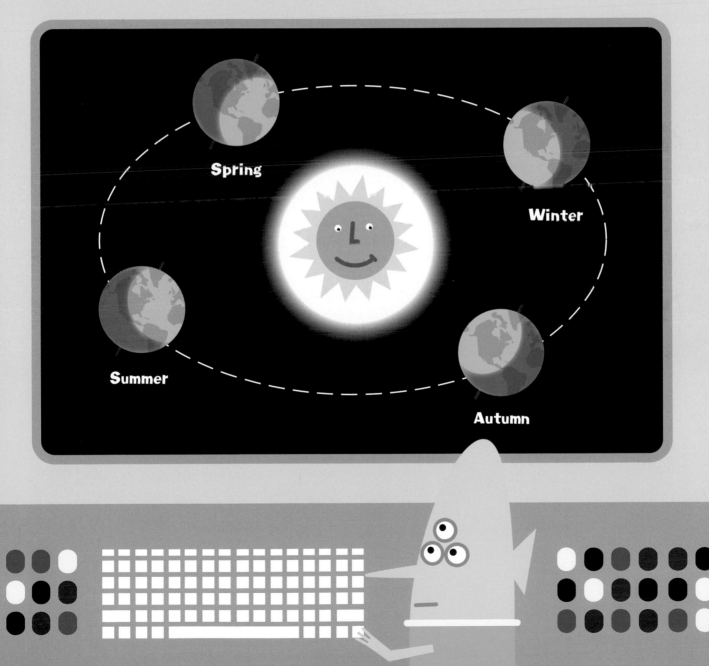

FUN PROJECT:
Why We Need Time Zones

Here's something you can do to help you understand why when it's noon on one side of the world, it's midnight on the other side.

Using a lamp and a globe in a darkened room, you can see how the turning Earth means it's morning on one side of the world and evening on the other side. If you don't have a globe, use a beach ball.

Turn on the lamp. Place the globe or ball near the lamp. If the lamp is the only source of light in the room, one side of the globe or ball—the side facing the lamp—will be in the light. The other side of the globe or ball will be dark.

Slowly turn the globe or ball. As the lighted side moves out of the light, the other side moves into the light. If you're using a globe, find the Atlantic Ocean. Shine the light directly on it. Since the earth turns in an easterly direction, as the globe turns, the sun first shines directly on the east coast of the United States: the side of the country from Maine to Florida.

Now slowly turn the globe to the right so as it turns, the light moves toward the Pacific Ocean. As you turn the globe, the light that was shining directly on New York City, Philadelphia, and Atlanta is soon shining directly on Chicago, New Orleans, and Houston. Keep slowly turning the globe. Soon the light is directly on Denver, Albuquerque, and Billings. Then it's shining on Phoenix, Las Vegas, and Los Angeles.

If you keep turning the globe, the light will soon be shining on Alaska. Then it will be shining on Hawaii. When it is shining directly on Shanghai, China, the east coast of the United States will be dark. When it's noon in Shanghai, it's midnight in Miami.

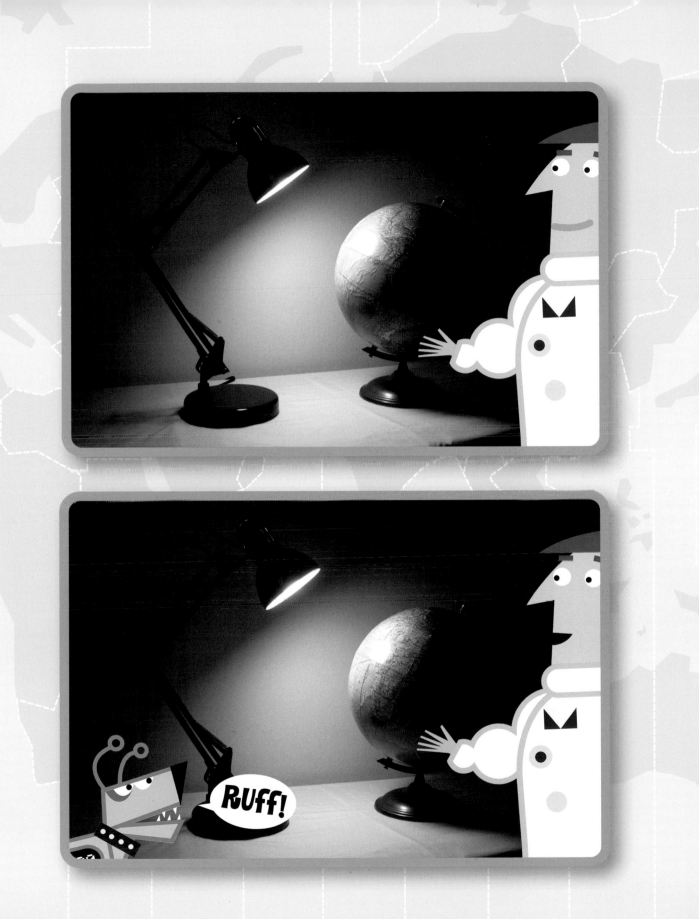

For Pam Glauber, an always cheerful,
helpful, and insightful editor
—D. A. A.

To my great-niece, Ariana
—E. M.

The publisher wishes to thank Tanya Buckingham, Assistant Director of the University of
Wisconsin-Madison, University of Wisconsin Cartography Lab, for her expert review of this book.

Text copyright © 2010 by David A. Adler
Illustrations copyright © 2010 by Edward Miller
All Rights Reserved
HOLIDAY HOUSE is registered in the U.S. Patent and Trademark Office.
Printed and bound in March 2011 at Tien Wah Press, Johor Bahru, Johor, Malaysia.
www.holidayhouse.com

3 5 7 9 10 8 6 4 2

Library of Congress Cataloging-in-Publication Data

Adler, David A.
Time zones / by David A. Adler. — 1st ed.
p. cm.
ISBN 978-0-8234-2201-2 (hardcover)
1. Time measurements—Juvenile literature. 2. Time—Systems and standards—
Juvenile literature. I. Title.
QB209.5.A35 2010
389'.17—dc22
2009007733

ISBN 978-0-8234-2385-9 (paperback)

Visit **www.davidaadler.com** for more information on the author, for a list of his books, and to download teacher's guides and
educational materials. You can also learn more about the writing process, take fun quizzes, and read select pages from David A. Adler's books.

Visit **www.edmiller.com** for activities that accompany this book. Become a fan of the **Edward Miller's Bookatorium** on Facebook.